First Station

Jesus Must Die

We adore You, O Christ, and we Bless you,
Because by your holy cross you have redeemed the world.

I think of Jesus: See Jesus is standing before Pilate.
"Some soldiers are with Him.
"You must die on a cross, Jesus." Pilate says

I talk to Jesus: Dear Jesus, Pilate does not know that you are God,
but I know that you are. You are the God who made Pilate and me.
You did not run away when Pilate said that you must die.
You wanted to die for my sins.

I love you Jesus, help me to never sin again.

Our Father who art in Heaven, hallowed be thy name,
thy kingdom come thy will be done on earth as it is in heaven.
Give us this day our daily bread and forgive us our trespasses
as we forgive those who trespass against us
and lead us not into temptation but deliver us from evil.
Amen

Hail Mary Full of Grace, the Lord is with you,
blessed are you amongst women and blessed is the fruit of your womb
Jesus. Holy Mary mother of God pray for us sinners now
and at the hour of our death.
Amen

Lord Jesus Crucified, have mercy on us

Second Station

Jesus Takes His Cross

We adore You, O Christ, and we Bless you,
Because by your holy cross you have redeemed the world.

I think of Jesus: See how happy Jesus is to see the big cross.
It is the key that will open Heaven for us.
Jesus takes the cross in His arms and kisses it.

I talk to Jesus: Jesus, you think of me when you see the cross.
Help me to remember how much you love me when I see you on the
cross. I have been a naughty child. Forgive me, Jesus.

I love you Jesus, help me to never sin again.

Our Father who art in heaven, hallowed be thy name,
thy kingdom come thy will be done on earth as it is in heaven.
Give us this day our daily bread and forgive us our trespasses
as we forgive those who trespass against us
and lead us not into temptation but deliver us from evil.
Amen

Hail Mary Full of Grace, the Lord is with you,
blessed are you amongst women and blessed is the fruit of your
womb Jesus. Holy Mary mother of God pray for us sinners now
and at the hour of our death.
Amen

Lord Jesus Crucified, have mercy on us

Third Station

Jesus Falls the First Time

We adore You, O Christ, and we Bless you,
Because by your holy cross you have redeemed the world.

I think of Jesus: Oh, see poor Jesus under the big cross.
Sins made the cross so heavy that Jesus fell.

I talk to Jesus: Jesus, I want to help you carry the cross.
I will be brave when you send me pain.
I will think of how much pain you are going through when you fall under
the cross.

I love you Jesus, help me to never sin again.

Our Father who art in heaven, hallowed be thy name,
thy kingdom come thy will be done on earth as it is in heaven.
Give us this day our daily bread and forgive us our trespasses
as we forgive those who trespass against us
and lead us not into temptation but deliver us from evil.
Amen

Hail Mary Full of Grace, the Lord is with you,
blessed are you amongst women and blessed is the fruit of your
womb Jesus. Holy Mary mother of God pray for us sinners now
and at the hour of our death.
Amen

Lord Jesus Crucified, have mercy on us

Fourth Station

Jesus Meets His Mother

We adore You, O Christ, and we Bless you,
Because by your holy cross you have redeemed the world.

I think of Jesus: Blessed Mother is very sad when she sees Jesus.
He has blood and dirt all over him. He does not look like her Boy, Jesus.

I talk to Jesus: Dear Jesus, I know how happy you were to see your
mother. You love Mary and were good to her.
I love my mother and I will be good to her, too.

I love you Jesus, help me to never sin again.

Our Father who art in heaven, hallowed be thy name,
thy kingdom come thy will be done on earth as it is in heaven.
Give us this day our daily bread and forgive us our trespasses
as we forgive those who trespass against us
and lead us not into temptation but deliver us from evil.
Amen

Hail Mary Full of Grace, the Lord is with you,
blessed are you amongst women and blessed is the fruit of your
womb Jesus. Holy Mary mother of God pray for us sinners now
and at the hour of our death.
Amen

Lord Jesus Crucified, have mercy on us

Fifth Station

Simon Helps Jesus

We adore You, O Christ, and we Bless you,
Because by your holy cross you have redeemed the world.

I think of Jesus: The soldiers make Simon help Jesus carry the cross.
Jesus blesses Simon. The cross is light for Simon to carry.

I talk to Jesus: Simon knows and loves you now, Jesus.
I want to help you carry the cross.
I will pray for poor sinners so they will know how much you love them.

.

I love you Jesus, help me to never sin again.

Our Father who art in heaven, hallowed be thy name,
thy kingdom come thy will be done on earth as it is in heaven.
Give us this day our daily bread and forgive us our trespasses
as we forgive those who trespass against us
and lead us not into temptation but deliver us from evil.
Amen

Hail Mary Full of Grace, the Lord is with you,
blessed are you amongst women and blessed is the fruit of your
womb Jesus. Holy Mary mother of God pray for us sinners now
and at the hour of our death.
Amen

Lord Jesus Crucified, have mercy on us

Sixth Station

Veronica wipes the Face of Jesus

We adore You, O Christ, and we Bless you,
Because by your holy cross you have redeemed the world.

I think of Jesus: Veronica gives Jesus a towel to wipe His face.
Jesus gives Veronica a surprise.
The towel has a picture of Jesus on it.

I talk to Jesus: Dear Jesus, I have more than your picture in my soul.
You are there Jesus, with Sanctifying Grace. Help me to keep my soul
pure and holy. Let me die rather than lose Sanctifying Grace.

I love you Jesus, help me to never sin again.

Our Father who art in heaven, hallowed be thy name,
thy kingdom come thy will be done on earth as it is in heaven.
Give us this day our daily bread and forgive us our trespasses
as we forgive those who trespass against us
and lead us not into temptation but deliver us from evil.
Amen

Hail Mary Full of Grace, the Lord is with you,
blessed are you amongst women and blessed is the fruit of your
womb Jesus. Holy Mary mother of God pray for us sinners now
and at the hour of our death.
Amen

Lord Jesus Crucified, have mercy on us

Seventh Station

Jesus falls the Second Time

We adore You, O Christ, and we Bless you,
Because by your holy cross you have redeemed the world.

I think of Jesus: Jesus falls again. He is tired of carrying the heavy cross.
The soldiers hit Jesus. Poor Jesus is thinking of me.

I talk to Jesus: Jesus, how it hurt you to fall again. My sins made you fall
under the cross. Every time I am naughty and hit someone,
I am like the soldiers who hit you.
Forgive me, Jesus.

I love you Jesus, help me to never sin again.

Our Father who art in heaven, hallowed be thy name,
thy kingdom come thy will be done on earth as it is in heaven.
Give us this day our daily bread and forgive us our trespasses
as we forgive those who trespass against us
and lead us not into temptation but deliver us from evil.
Amen

Hail Mary Full of Grace, the Lord is with you,
blessed are you amongst women and blessed is the fruit of your
womb Jesus. Holy Mary mother of God pray for us sinners now
and at the hour of our death.
Amen

Lord Jesus Crucified, have mercy on us

Eighth Station

Jesus Talks to the Holy Women

We adore You, O Christ, and we Bless you,
Because by your holy cross you have redeemed the world.

I think of Jesus: Jesus sees women who are crying.
They love Jesus and are going up the hill with Him.
Jesus says, "Do not cry for Me, but for your sins."

I talk to Jesus: I am sorry for my sins, Jesus. Dear Jesus, you talk to me through the priest. Every time I go to confession, you forgive my sins when I am sorry. I thank you for this big present.

I love you Jesus, help me to never sin again.

Our Father who art in heaven, hallowed be thy name,
thy kingdom come thy will be done on earth as it is in heaven.
Give us this day our daily bread and forgive us our trespasses
as we forgive those who trespass against us
and lead us not into temptation but deliver us from evil.
Amen

Hail Mary Full of Grace, the Lord is with you,
blessed are you amongst women and blessed is the fruit of your
womb Jesus. Holy Mary mother of God pray for us sinners
now and at the hour of our death.
Amen

Lord Jesus Crucified, have mercy on us

Ninth Station

Jesus Falls the Third Time

We adore You, O Christ, and we Bless you,
Because by your holy cross you have redeemed the world.

I think of Jesus: Jesus falls again. This time He falls to the ground.
The soldiers hurt Jesus.

I talk to Jesus: The soldiers hurt you, Jesus, but I hurt you too, when I commit a sin. I will try to make up for it by thinking of you every time I see you on the cross.

I love you Jesus, help me to never sin again.

Our Father who art in heaven, hallowed be thy name,
thy kingdom come thy will be done on earth as it is in heaven.
Give us this day our daily bread and forgive us our trespasses
as we forgive those who trespass against us
and lead us not into temptation but deliver us from evil.
Amen

Hail Mary Full of Grace, the Lord is with you,
blessed are you amongst women and blessed is the fruit of your
womb Jesus. Holy Mary mother of God pray for us sinners now
and at the hour of our death.
Amen

Lord Jesus Crucified, have mercy on us

Tenth Station

The Soldiers Take off Jesus' Clothes

We adore You, O Christ, and we Bless you,
Because by your holy cross you have redeemed the world.

I think of Jesus: See how the soldiers are pulling off poor Jesus' clothes. That made all His sores hurt again. Jesus is thinking of me.

I talk to Jesus: Dear Jesus, how the soldiers hurt you. I hurt you when I am mean to my friends, too.
You live in their souls, just as you live in mine. Forgive me, Jesus.

I love you Jesus, help me to never sin again.

Our Father who art in heaven, hallowed be thy name,
thy kingdom come thy will be done on earth as it is in heaven.
Give us this day our daily bread and forgive us our trespasses
as we forgive those who trespass against us
and lead us not into temptation but deliver us from evil.
Amen

Hail Mary Full of Grace, the Lord is with you,
blessed are you amongst women and blessed is the fruit of your
womb Jesus. Holy Mary mother of God pray for us sinners
now and at the hour of our death.
Amen

Lord Jesus Crucified, have mercy on us

Eleventh Station

Jesus is Nailed to the Cross

We adore You, O Christ, and we Bless you,
Because by your holy cross you have redeemed the world.

I think of Jesus: See Jesus lying on the cross.
The wood is so hard and cold. Jesus sees the nails and hammers ready to
put Him on the cross. Jesus wants to die for me.

I talk to Jesus: Jesus, it makes me sad when I see you lying on the cross.
You are so brave and strong. Help me to be brave like you, Jesus.

I love you Jesus, help me to never sin again.

Our Father who art in heaven, hallowed be thy name,
thy kingdom come thy will be done on earth as it is in heaven.
Give us this day our daily bread and forgive us our trespasses
as we forgive those who trespass against us
and lead us not into temptation but deliver us from evil.
Amen

Hail Mary Full of Grace, the Lord is with you,
blessed are you amongst women and blessed is the fruit of
your womb Jesus. Holy Mary mother of God pray for us sinners now
and at the hour of our death.
Amen

Lord Jesus Crucified, have mercy on us

Twelfth Station

Jesus Dies on the Cross

We adore You, O Christ, and we Bless you,
Because by your holy cross you have redeemed the world.

I think of Jesus: Look at Jesus. His arms are open to show me that he
loves me. Look at the big nails in His hands and feet.
How they hurt poor Jesus.

I talk to Jesus: Dear Jesus, here you are dying for me. You love me very
much. I love you too, Jesus. I am sorry for all of my sins, because they
hurt you. You are so good, Jesus.

I love you Jesus, help me to never sin again.

Our Father who art in heaven, hallowed be thy name,
thy kingdom come thy will be done on earth as it is in heaven.
Give us this day our daily bread and forgive us our trespasses
as we forgive those who trespass against us
and lead us not into temptation but deliver us from evil.
Amen

Hail Mary Full of Grace, the Lord is with you,
blessed are you amongst women and blessed is the fruit of
your womb Jesus. Holy Mary mother of God pray for us sinners now
and at the hour of our death.
Amen

Lord Jesus Crucified, have mercy on us

Thirteenth Station

Jesus is Taken Down from the Cross

We adore You, O Christ, and we Bless you,
Because by your holy cross you have redeemed the world.

I think of Jesus: Jesus is dead now. He died to open Heaven with the
new key, the cross. Jesus is in His Mother's arms.

I talk to Jesus: Dear Jesus, I thank you for dying on the cross for me.
I will show you how much I love you for doing this for me.
You obeyed your Father in heaven.
I will obey at home and in school, too.

I love you Jesus, help me to never sin again.

Our Father who art in heaven, hallowed be thy name,
thy kingdom come thy will be done on earth as it is in heaven.
Give us this day our daily bread and forgive us our trespasses
as we forgive those who trespass against us
and lead us not into temptation but deliver us from evil.
Amen

Hail Mary Full of Grace, the Lord is with you,
blessed are you amongst women and blessed is the fruit of
your womb Jesus. Holy Mary mother of God pray for us sinners now
and at the hour of our death.
Amen

Lord Jesus Crucified, have mercy on us

Fourteenth Station

Jesus is Laid in the Tomb

We adore You, O Christ, and we Bless you,
Because by your holy cross you have redeemed the world.

I think of Jesus: Now they are putting Jesus into the grave.
He is finished with His long hard trip to the hill of Calvary.

I talk to Jesus: Dear Jesus, your body is cold and dead now.
I know that you will surprise everybody when you return to life.
Help me to remember that you suffered to help me get to Heaven.

I love you Jesus, help me to never sin again.

Our Father who art in heaven, hallowed be thy name,
thy kingdom come thy will be done on earth as it is in heaven.
Give us this day our daily bread and forgive us our trespasses
as we forgive those who trespass against us
and lead us not into temptation but deliver us from evil.
Amen

Hail Mary Full of Grace, the Lord is with you,
blessed are you amongst women and blessed is the fruit of your
womb Jesus. Holy Mary mother of God pray for us sinners now
and at the hour of our death.
Amen

Lord Jesus Crucified, have mercy on us

Prayer after stations

Dear Jesus, I thank you again for suffering and dying for me.
I will be good and try to help someone love you better.
I thank you, Jesus.

Dear Jesus, have mercy on the souls in Purgatory.

Our Father who art in heaven, hallowed be thy name,
thy kingdom come thy will be done on earth as it is in heaven.
Give us this day our daily bread and forgive us our trespasses
as we forgive those who trespass against us
and lead us not into temptation but deliver us from evil.
Amen

Hail Mary Full of Grace, the Lord is with you,
blessed are you amongst women and blessed is the fruit of your
womb Jesus. Holy Mary mother of God pray for us sinners now
and at the hour of our death.
Amen

Glory be to the Father and to the Son and to the Holy Ghost,
as it was in the beginning, is now and ever shall be,
world without end.
Amen

CPSIA information can be obtained
at www.ICGtesting.com
Printed in the USA
LVHW012253190521
687904LV00013B/681

9 780645 022087